Schofield & Sims KS1 SATs Practice Papers

Maths

English

Notes and answers

Test guides
Mark schemes
Marking guidance

Schofield & Sims

About the KS1 SATs Maths and English Practice Papers

The *KS1 SATs Practice Papers* will support your child to prepare for the SATs in maths and English that they will take towards the end of Year 2. Each paper has been carefully written to closely resemble the language and question types found in the SATs papers.

The *KS1 SATs Practice Papers* are designed to be used in the immediate run-up to the tests, to help your child become familiar with the formats and approximate timings of the real papers. (Please note that at Key Stage 1, the SATs are not strictly timed.)

Overview of the Practice Papers in this pack

Maths – Paper 1: arithmetic	
Number of questions	25
Number of marks available	25
Time allowed	Approximately 20 minutes

Maths – Paper 2: reasoning	
Number of questions	31
Number of marks available	35
Time allowed	Approximately 35 minutes, including aural questions

English – reading: Paper 1	
Number of questions	20
Number of marks available	20
Time allowed	Approximately 30 minutes

English – reading: Paper 2	
Reading booklet	3 reading extracts: 1 fiction, 1 poem, 1 non-fiction
Number of questions	18
Number of marks available	20
Time allowed	Approximately 40 minutes

English – grammar, punctuation and spelling (GPS) Paper 1: spelling	
Number of questions	20
Number of marks available	20
Time allowed	Approximately 15 minutes

English – grammar, punctuation and spelling (GPS) Paper 2: grammar and punctuation	
Number of questions	19
Number of marks available	20
Time allowed	Approximately 20 minutes

Contents

Guide to the maths papers

Administering the papers

- Ensure that your child has a quiet area in which to work, with no distractions.

- Provide any equipment they may need such as a pen, pencil, eraser, mirror and ruler.

- Although erasers are allowed in the SATs, it is best to encourage your child to cross out any answers they would like to change. Please note that calculators, tracing paper and number apparatus are not permitted in the SATs.

- Although the KS1 SATs are not strictly timed, it is a good idea to use the approximate times given for each test as a guideline.

- It is best to complete the papers in the order in which they appear in this pack. However, your child should not try to do all of the papers in one session; they should have a break between tests.

Instructions for Maths Paper 1: arithmetic

- Give your child the paper and help them to fill in the cover page. Explain that there are 25 questions to answer.

- Start with the practice question on page 2 of the question paper. You can work through this question with your child.

- Your child should try to answer all of the questions. If they are unable to answer a question, they should move on to the next question and come back to it later.

- If your child makes a mistake, they should cross or rub it out and then write their new answer clearly.

- The arithmetic paper is expected to take around 20 minutes, but it is not strictly timed. Use your own judgement to decide when your child is ready to stop the test.

Instructions for Maths Paper 2: reasoning

- Give your child the paper and help them to fill in the cover page. Explain that there are 31 questions to answer.

- The practice question and the first five test questions are aural questions. You should read these questions aloud using the script on page 5 of this booklet.

- Start with the practice question on page 2 of the question paper. After the fifth question, explain that for the rest of the paper, the questions will be written in the booklet. Explain to your child that they must show their working out if the question asks them to. They may get an extra mark for it.

- Your child should try to answer all of the questions. If they are unable to answer a question, they should move on to the next question and come back to it later.

- If your child makes a mistake, they should cross or rub it out and then write their new answer clearly.

- The reasoning paper is expected to take around 35 minutes, but it is not strictly timed. Use your own judgement to decide when your child is ready to stop the test.

Aural questions in Maths Paper 2: reasoning

Read the questions below aloud. Say the bold part twice and leave a gap of a couple of seconds between each question. Explain that the first question is a practice question.

Wait until your child has answered the question before you go on to the next one. Help your child to locate each question if necessary.

Question	Script
P	**Practice question** **Look at the berries. How many raspberries are there?** Write your answer in the box.
1	**Question one** **Write one more than eight.** Write your answer in the box.
2	**Question two** **Write the number five in words.** Write your answer in the box.
3	**Question three** **Add these three numbers together.** **3 8 2** Write your answer in the box.
4	**Question four** **What number must Tom add to fifteen to get an answer of twenty-four?** Write your answer in the box.
5	**Question five** **How many days are there in one week?** Write your answer in the box.

Maths content domains

The number at the beginning of each maths content domain code represents the year in which this content is taught. The letter in the code represents the subject area, as listed below.

Number		Measurement, geometry and statistics	
N	Number and place value	M	Measurement
C	Addition, subtraction, multiplication, division (calculations)	G	Geometry – properties of shapes
F	Fractions	P	Geometry – position and direction
		S	Statistics

Marking grid

Please find below a marking grid for you to record your child's scores. For the maths answers and mark schemes, turn to pages 7 to 13 of this booklet.

Paper	Maximum score available	Your child's score
Paper 1: arithmetic	25	
Paper 2: reasoning	35	
Total score	**60**	

Scaled scores and the expected standard

Test papers vary a little in difficulty from year to year. To take this into account, SATs paper 'raw' scores are always converted into scaled scores. This allows an accurate comparison of performance over time.

To view the government's 2019 SATs score conversion table, visit:
gov.uk/government/publications/2019-scaled-scores-at-key-stage-1

Pupils need to achieve a minimum scaled score of 100 to achieve the expected standard in the Key Stage 1 SATs papers. In 2019, pupils needed to achieve 34 out of 60 to achieve the expected standard for maths (a scaled score of 100).

Answers

Question	Content domain	Answer	Marks
Practice question	1C2a	8 + 8 = **16**	**0m**
1	1C1	4 + 3 = **7**	1m
2	1N1b	10 + 10 + 10 = **30**	1m
3	1C1	17 − 7 = **10**	1m
4	2C2b	26 + 10 = **36**	1m
5	1N2b	19 − 5 = **14**	1m
6	2N6	6 + 2 + 4 = **12**	1m
7	2C2b	57 − 4 = **53**	1m
8	2C2b	37 + 6 = **43**	1m
9	2C2b	43 − 27 = **16** If using the standard written method of subtraction (sometimes known as decomposition), children will need to exchange 1 ten from the 4 tens so that 7 ones can be subtracted from 13 (rather than 3) ones.	1m
10	2N6	78 − 30 = **48**	1m
11	2C2b	60 − 16 = **44** If using the standard written method of subtraction, children will need to exchange 1 ten from the 6 tens so that 6 ones can be subtracted from 10 (rather than 0) ones.	1m
12	2C6	6 × 5 = **30** Children could also solve the calculation pictorially: 	1m
13	2C2b	84 − 33 = **51**	1m
14	2C6	100 ÷ 10 = **10** Encourage your child to use their known times tables facts to help them solve division questions. For example, 10 multiplied by what number equals 100?	1m
15	2C3	**5** + 4 = 9 If your child gave the answer 13, encourage them to notice that if 4 were added to 13 the answer would be 17, not 9. Point out that the missing number must be 4 *less* than 9, which can be found by subtracting 4 from 9.	1m

Answers

Question	Content domain	Answer	Marks
16	2C3	**19** + 7 = 26 If your child gave the answer 33, explain that if 7 were added to 33 the answer would be 40, not 26. Point out that the missing number must be 7 *less* than 26, which can be found by subtracting 7 from 26.	1m
17	2F1b	$\frac{1}{2}$ of 26 = **13**	1m
18	2F1a	$\frac{3}{4}$ of 20 = **15** Three-quarters can be found by first dividing by 4 to find one-quarter and then multiplying by 3 to find three-quarters. Using the bar model to show this pictorially may help your child's understanding: XXX XX | XXX XX | XXX XX | XXX XX	1m
19	2C3	73 − **32** = 41	1m
20	2C3	60 − **40** = 20	1m
21	2C2b	58 + 27 = **85** If using the standard written method of addition, children will need to carry 1 ten across from the ones as 8 + 7 = 15. This ten is then added to the 5 tens and 2 tens that are already in the tens column.	1m
22	2C2b	1 + 8 + 7 = **16** Remind children that the numbers can be added in any order for addition.	1m
23	2F1a	$\frac{1}{3}$ of 18 = **6** One third of a number is found by dividing it by 3. Using the bar model to show this pictorially may help your child's understanding: XXX XXX | XXX XXX | XXX XXX	1m
24	2C6	50 ÷ 5 = **10** Encourage your child to use their known times tables facts to help them solve division questions. For example, 5 multiplied by what number equals 50?	1m
25	2C2b	68 − 19 = **49** If using the standard written method of subtraction, children need to exchange 1 ten from the 6 tens so that 9 ones can be subtracted from 18 (rather than 8) ones.	1m

End of Maths Paper 1 mark scheme

Answers

Question	Content domain	Answer	Marks	Marking guidance
Practice question	1N2a	**4 berries**	**0m**	
1	1N2b	**9**	**1m**	Accept answer in numerals (9) or words (nine).
2	1N2c	**Five**	**1m**	Only accept the answer written in words.
3	2C2a	**13** Encourage your child to use their understanding of number bonds when adding three numbers together. 3 + 8 + 2 It would be efficient to add 8 + 2 to make 10 and then add 3.	**1m**	
4	2C3	**9** This can be answered by either counting on from 15 to 24 (addition) or counting back from 24 to 15 (subtraction).	**1m**	
5	1M4c	**7 days**	**1m**	
6	2N3/ 2N4	**12** *or* **14** Your child should notice that the only two-digit numbers they can make that are less than 15 are 12 and 14. Encourage your child to use their knowledge of place value when answering a question like this. Ask if the number has to be less than 15, then what card must be in the tens column? What cards can then be used for the ones column?	**1m**	
7	1C1	**5** A child sometimes sees the equals sign as an instruction to do something rather than as a sign of equality (i.e. that things on either side of it should be equal). As a result, your child may be confused that there is not simply an answer to the right of it. Show your child that 20 – 10 equals 10 and 15 – 5 also equals 10.	**1m**	

Answers

Question	Content domain	Answer	Marks	Marking guidance
8	2N2b	**27, 36, 41, 60** If your child has answered this question incorrectly, they may not fully understand the place value of digits in a number (tens and ones) – for example, that the 6 in 36 is worth less than the 6 in 60.	1m	Do not award a mark if the digits of any number are transposed or if any of the numbers are out of order.
9	2C1/ 2C2a	**£17** This can be answered by counting on from £28 to £45 (addition) or subtracting £28 from £45 using a mental method or written calculation.	1m	
10	2C8	**25 pencils** This question can be solved using repeated addition: 5 + 5 + 5 + 5 + 5. Encourage your child to understand that this is the same as 5×5.	1m	
11	2C6	**⑮** Here your child must look to see which number is incorrectly placed in the Carroll diagram. A knowledge of odd and even numbers is necessary.	1m	Award the mark if the number 15 has been indicated in some other way, for example written at the side or ticked.
12	2N1	**26, 46** Your child should notice that there is a pattern in the numbers given: they increase by 10. When counting on in tens, the ones digit always stays the same.	1m	
13	1F1a	**7 biscuits**	1m	Also accept the correct number of biscuits circled. If your child has written a digit in reverse (for example, the reflection of 7), award the mark, provided that it clearly shows the characteristics of a 7 rather than a 2.
14	2C8	**60 sweets** This can be solved using multiplication (6 lots of 10 or 6×10) or addition (counting on in tens).	1m	

Answers

Question	Content domain	Answer	Marks	Marking guidance
15	2M3a	**Star and Two scoops** Your child may use trial and error for this question. They may notice that the 'One scoop' ice cream costs 40p and, when added to any other ice cream, will give an amount ending in 5p.	1m	
16	2C1	**20, 30**	1m	
17	2M2	**450ml** Establish that the scale is counting up in increments of 100ml. The level of the juice is half way between 400ml and 500ml.	1m	
18	2N2b	(38) ◯ ◯ ◯ ◯ (43) (44) (45) Your child needs to be able to count back from the numbers in the sequence.	1m	
19a	2S21	**10 ice creams** One symbol on the chart stands for 5 items.	Up to 2m	Award **1 mark** for each correct answer.
19b	2S2b	Sunday 🍦		
20	2M2	Make sure that your child is using a ruler properly.	1m	
21	2M9	**25p** 20p + 20p = 40p 40p + 15p = 55p 80p − 55p = 25p	Up to 2m	If the answer is incorrect, award **1 mark** for an appropriate method.
22	2C8	**5 strawberries**	1m	Award the mark if the child has shown this pictorially:

Answers

Question	Content domain	Answer	Marks	Marking guidance
23	2F1b	**16, 8, 4** Remind your child that half can be found by dividing by 2.	**1m**	
24	2M4a	quarter to eleven ☑	**1m**	Accept answer ticked or crossed but ensure there is clear indication of one correct answer only.
25	2P2	**left 2, down 4, right 3, up 6, right 2**	**Up to 2m**	Award only **1 mark** if one of the instructions is incorrect. Do not award a mark if more than one instruction is incorrect.
26	2N4	**28** Split the line in half and then in half again to help your child estimate.	**1m**	
27	2G2b	☑	**1m**	Accept answer ticked or crossed, but ensure there is clear indication of one correct answer only.
28	2C6/ 2C8	**2** **10** Encourage your child to use their times table facts when solving division calculations. For example, 3 multiplied by what number equals 30?	**1m**	Both correct answers are needed for the award of **1 mark**.
29	2C4	**29 cupcakes** 65 − 36 = 29	**1m**	
30	2C6/ 2C4	**60g** Mass of two balls = 35g + 35g = 70g Mass of feather = 35g − 25g = 10g So the mass of the toy car = 60g (70g − 10g).	**Up to 2m**	If the answer is incorrect, award **1 mark** for an appropriate method.

Answers

Question	Content domain	Answer	Marks	Marking guidance
31	2C4	◯ = 2 ▢ = 8 Encourage your child to start a logical puzzle by looking for one unknown. We know 3 circles is equal to 6. 6 ÷ 3 = 2 so the value of one circle is 2. Circle + Square = 10 so 2 + Square = 10. Your child can use number bonds to calculate 2 + 8 = 10.	1m	Both correct values are needed for the award of **1 mark**.

End of Maths Paper 2 mark scheme

Guide to the reading papers

Administering the papers

- Ensure that your child has a quiet area in which to work, with no distractions.

- Provide any equipment they may need such as a pen or pencil and eraser.

- Although erasers are allowed in the SATs, it is best to encourage your child to cross out any answers they would like to change. Please note that dictionaries are not permitted in the SATs.

- Although the KS1 SATs are not strictly timed, it is a good idea to use the approximate times given for each test as a guideline.

- It is best to complete the papers in the order in which they appear in this pack. However, your child should not try to do all of the papers in one session; they should have a break between tests.

Instructions for Reading: Paper 1

- In **Reading: Paper 1**, reading texts and questions are in the same booklet. The paper contains one fiction text (*The Blue Jackal*) and one non-fiction text (*Penguins*).

- Give your child the paper and help them to fill in the cover page. Explain that there are 20 questions to answer.

- Start with the list of 'Useful words' and the practice questions on pages 4–5 of the test paper. Read these pages with your child, discussing the meaning of each word and working through each practice question. When your child has completed the first section, follow the same steps with the 'Useful words' and practice questions on pages 14–15, which introduce the second section of the paper.

- For most questions, your child will write their answer on a line or choose the right answer and tick the box next to it. For other questions, they will put numbers in boxes to order events or draw lines to match answers.

- Your child should try to answer all of the questions. If they are unable to answer a question, they should move on to the next question and come back to it later.

- If your child makes a mistake, they should cross or rub it out and then write their new answer clearly.

- The paper is expected to take around 30 minutes, but it is not strictly timed. Use your own judgement to decide when your child is ready to stop the test.

Instructions for Reading: Paper 2

- In **Reading: Paper 2**, there is a separate **Reading booklet** to use with the question paper. This contains a fiction text (*The Cloud-Eater*), a poem (*On the bridge*) and a non-fiction text (*Tomatoes*).

- Give your child the paper and help them to fill in the cover page. Explain that there are 18 questions to answer.

- Point out that each question includes the page in the Reading booklet where the answer can be found. Your child should look out for this information in brackets at the end of each question.

- As in **Reading: Paper 1**, for most questions, your child will write their answer on a line or choose the right answer and tick the box next to it. For other questions, they may need to tick to show if a statement is true or false; number statements in order; fill in tables with information or draw lines to match answers.

- Your child should try to answer all of the questions. If they are unable to answer a question, they should move on to the next question and come back to it later.

- If your child makes a mistake, they should cross or rub it out and then write their new answer clearly.

- The paper is expected to take around 40 minutes, but it is not strictly timed. Use your own judgement to decide when your child is ready to stop the test.

Reading content domains

The number at the beginning of each reading content domain code represents the Key Stage (1 or 2).
At Key Stage 1, there are five content domain codes for reading, which are summarised below. In the KS1 SATs, most questions will have a single content domain code. Occasionally, two content domain codes are relevant.

Content domain references for reading	
1a	draw on knowledge of vocabulary to understand texts
1b	identify/explain key aspects of fiction and non-fiction texts, such as characters, events, titles and information
1c	identify and explain the sequence of events in texts
1d	make inferences from the text
1e	predict what might happen on the basis of what has been read so far

Marking grid

Please find below a marking grid for you to use to record your child's score. For the reading answers and mark schemes, turn to pages 16 to 21 of this booklet.

Paper	Maximum score available	Your child's score
Reading: Paper 1	20	
Reading: Paper 2	20	
Total score	**40**	

Scaled scores and the expected standard

Test papers vary a little in difficulty from year to year. To take this into account, SATs paper 'raw' scores are always converted into scaled scores. This allows an accurate comparison of performance over time.

To view the government's 2019 SATs score conversion table, visit:
gov.uk/government/publications/2019-scaled-scores-at-key-stage-1

Pupils need to achieve a minimum scaled score of 100 to achieve the expected standard in the Key Stage 1 SATs papers. In 2019, pupils needed to achieve 25 out of 40 to achieve the expected standard for reading (a scaled score of 100).

Answers

Question	Content domain	Answer	Marks
Practice question a	1b	he was looking for food ☑	0m
Practice question b	1b	• **midnight** Also accept: night time	0m
1	1b	Award **1 mark** for an answer that refers to food or something to eat.	1m
2	1b	Award **1 mark** for: under the window ☑	1m
3	1b, 1d	Award **1 mark** for answers that refer to what the jackal said/thought, for example: • he didn't look like a jackal anymore • he thought the others would laugh at him • he thought he looked silly	1m
4	1a	Award **1 mark** for: • terror	1m
5	1d	Award **1 mark** for: pleased ☑	1m
6	1b	Award **1 mark** for: • they bowed down Also accept: they said, 'You are our king!'	1m
7	1d, 1a	Award **1 mark** for an explanation that refers to the effect of the blue colour on the other animals, for example: • they thought the colour made him special • they thought it was the colour of kings • the colour gave him power over the other animals Also accept reference to what the jackal said, e.g. he said blue is the colour of kings.	1m

Answers

Question	Content domain	Answer	Marks
8	1b	Award **1 mark** for all correctly matched. lions — found his food mice — gave him water elephants — fanned him monkeys — fetched grass for his bed	1m
9	1d	Award **1 mark** for an explanation referring to the other jackals knowing the truth, for example: • they knew/would know he was just a jackal • they would tell the other animals his secret/he was just a jackal	1m
10	1b	Award **1 mark** for: he was treated too well ✓	1m
11	1a	Award **1 mark** for: not special ✓	1m
12	1d	Award **1 mark** for: he pretended to be something he was not ✓	1m
13	1c	Award **1 mark** for the correct order. the jackal returned to the forest 2 the jackal's fur was dyed blue 1 the jackal was chased out of the forest 4 the jackal tricked the other animals 3	1m

Answers

Question	Content domain	Answer	Marks
Practice question c	1b	• **Antarctic** Also accept: in a land of snow and ice	0m
Practice question d	1b, 1a	swim ☑	0m
14	1b	Award **1 mark** for: to help them slide ☑	1m
15	1b	Award **1 mark** for **both** of the following: • fat/a layer of fat/(fat) tummy or belly • feathers/waterproof feathers/layers of feathers	1m
16	1a	Award **1 mark** for: spiky ☑	1m
17	1b	Award **1 mark** for an answer that refers to catching food, for example: • to catch their food • because they catch all their food underwater • because they need to catch fish to eat	1m
18	1b	Award **1 mark** for: Emperor penguins lay eggs in spring. ☑	1m
19	1d	Award **1 mark** for an answer that refers to keeping it warm, for example: • to keep it warm • because it would be too cold on the ice	1m
20	1a	Award **1 mark** for: • cosy Also accept: tucked	1m

End of English reading Paper 1 mark scheme

Answers

Question	Content domain	Answer	Marks
1	1d	Award **1 mark** for answers referring to being close to clouds, for example: • because he liked eating clouds • because that's where there are lots of clouds • so he could catch clouds in his mouth	1m
2	1a	Award **1 mark** for **both** of the following: • baked [hard] • scorched **Do not** accept 'shrivelled' as this describes the crops, not the ground.	1m
3	1b	Award **1 mark** for a reason/motive found in the text, for example: • because he wanted to make the people happy • because his grandmother was sad • because he heard the sorrow in his grandmother's voice • because he wanted to help the village/the people	1m
4	1d, 1b	Award **1 mark** for reasons that can be inferred from the text, for example: • because he was going to do something brave/difficult • because he was very brave to try to kill the Cloud-Eater • because he was volunteering when no one else would • because he was doing something to help the people	1m
5	1d	Award **1 mark** for an answer that refers to the red feather, for example: • because he had the red feather • because his grandmother had given him the red feather	1m
6	1b, 1d	Award **1 mark** for reference to hearing the Cloud-Eater's heart beat, for example: • the boy could hear the Cloud-Eater's heart beating/hear his heart beat/came to a place they could hear his heart beating	1m

Answers

Question	Content domain	Answer	Marks
7	1b	Award **1 mark** for all correctly matched: the red feather — helped him find his way the blue feather — helped him speak to the gopher the yellow feather — helped him shrink in size the black feather — helped him fire the arrow	1m
8	1e	Award **1 mark** for a plausible prediction based on something in the text, for example: • I think everyone will cheer him • I think there will be a big celebration because it has started to rain • I think crops will grow again • I think his grandmother will be very proud of him • I think the people will give him a reward because he has saved them	1m
9	1d	Award **1 mark** for: over a river ✓	1m
10	1b	Award **1 mark** for **all three** of the following: • a [little] fish • a [water] rat • a spider	1m
11	1a	Award **1 mark** for: big ✓	1m
12	1b	Award **1 mark** for **each** of the following ideas (in any order). Idea 1: throw stones in the water and watch the circles they make (1 mark) Idea 2: make a boat out of a flower and watch it float away down the river (1 mark)	Up to 2m

Question	Content domain	Answer	Marks
13	1b	Award **1 mark** for reference to them being thought poisonous, for example: • because people thought they were poisonous Also accept: • because they grew them as decorative plants	1m
14	1d	Award **1 mark** for reference to them needing warmth, for example: • because it's too cold to grow them outside • because they need sun/warmth • because it is too cold in some countries/places	1m
15	1b, 1d	Award **1 mark** for **three** of the following: • in a salad • tomato juice • [sliced] in a sandwich • salsa • like a fruit	1m
16	1b	Award **1 mark** for: fish ✓	1m
17	1b	Award **1 mark** for reference to the food fight/throwing tomatoes	1m
18	1b	Award **1 mark** for **three** boxes ticked correctly; award **2 marks** for **all four** boxes ticked correctly.	Up to 2m

Sentence	True	False
Tomatoes are vegetables.		✓
The bright colours in tomatoes are good for you.	✓	
Today all tomatoes are red.		✓
Tomato leaves are not good to eat.	✓	

End of English reading Paper 2 mark scheme

Guide to the GPS papers

Administering the papers

- Ensure that your child has a quiet area in which to work, with no distractions.

- Provide any equipment they may need such as a pen or pencil and eraser.

- Although erasers are allowed in the SATs, it is best to encourage your child to cross out any answers they would like to change. Please note that dictionaries are not permitted in the SATs.

- Although the KS1 SATs are not strictly timed, it is a good idea to use the approximate times given for each test as a guideline.

- It is best to complete the papers in the order in which they appear in this pack. However, your child should not try to do all of the papers in one session; they should have a break between tests.

Instructions for GPS Paper 1: spelling

- **GPS Paper 1: spelling** is an aural spelling test. Use the script on page 24 to read the questions to your child.

- Give your child the paper and help them to fill in the cover page. Explain that the paper contains 20 different sentences, each with a word missing.

- Explain that you will read out the word, then the sentence, and then the word on its own again. Your child should fill in each missing word, being careful to spell it correctly.

- Help your child to do the practice question on page 2 to check that they understand what to do before you start the test.

- Leave a gap of several seconds between each spelling. You can repeat the target word if necessary.

- When you finish the last sentence, read all 20 spellings again.

- If your child makes a mistake, they should cross or rub it out and then write their new answer clearly.

- The paper is expected to take about 15 minutes, but it is not strictly timed. Use your own judgement to decide when your child is ready to stop the test.

Instructions for GPS Paper 2: grammar and punctuation

- **GPS Paper 2: grammar and punctuation** is a written test.

- Give your child the paper and help them to fill in the cover page. Explain that there are 19 questions to answer.

- On page 3 of the test paper, there are two practice questions. Help your child to answer these questions before they start the paper.

- For some questions, your child will need to tick a box, circle their answer or draw lines to match answers. For other questions, they will write a word, phrase or sentence on a line. Remind your child to read each question carefully and look for the key words that tell them what to do.

- Your child should try to answer all of the questions. If they are unable to answer a question, they should move on to the next question and come back to it later.

- If your child makes a mistake, they should cross or rub it out and then write their new answer clearly.

- The paper is expected to take about 20 minutes, but it is not strictly timed. Use your own judgement to decide when your child is ready to stop the test.

Grammar and punctuation content domains

There are six overarching content domain codes for grammar, which cover the following subject areas:

Content domain references for grammar and punctuation			
G1	grammatical terms/word classes	G4	verb tenses and consistency
G2	functions of sentences	G5	punctuation
G3	combining words, phrases and clauses	G6	vocabulary

Spelling content domains

The spelling content domain references (see pages 27 to 28) tell us the sound, spelling or type of the word being tested.

For full explanations of each grammar, punctuation and spelling content domain, visit:
gov.uk/government/publications/key-stage-1-english-grammar-punctuation-and-spelling-test-framework

Marking grid

Please find below a marking grid for you to use to record your child's scores. For the grammar, punctuation and spelling answers and mark schemes, turn to pages 27 to 31 of this booklet.

Paper	Maximum score available	Your child's score
Paper 1: spelling	20	
Paper 2: grammar and punctuation	20	
Total score	**40**	

Scaled scores and the expected standard

Test papers vary a little in difficulty from year to year. To take this into account, SATs paper 'raw' scores are always converted into scaled scores. This allows an accurate comparison of performance over time.

To view the government's 2019 SATs score conversion table, visit:
gov.uk/government/publications/2019-scaled-scores-at-key-stage-1

Pupils need to achieve a minimum scaled score of 100 to achieve the expected standard in the Key Stage 1 SATs papers. In 2019, pupils needed to achieve 24 out of 40 to achieve the expected standard for GPS (a scaled score of 100).

Spelling script

The spelling test should take about 15 minutes to complete. However, use this as an estimate and give your child as much time as they need to complete the test.

Explain that **GPS Paper 1: spelling** contains 20 different sentences, each with a word missing. Explain that you will read out the word, then the sentence, then the word on its own again. Your child should fill in each missing word, being careful to spell it correctly.

Leave at least 12 seconds between spellings. You can repeat the target word if necessary. When you finish the last sentence, read all 20 sentences again so that your child can check their work.

Help your child to do the practice question on page 2 of **GPS Paper 1: spelling** to check that they understand what to do before you start the test.

Practice spelling: The word is **park**.

I fed the ducks in the **park**.

The word is **park**.

Spelling 1: The word is **live**.

Some fish **live** in the sea.

The word is **live**.

Spelling 2: The word is **fizz**.

The drink began to **fizz**.

The word is **fizz**.

Spelling 3: The word is **large**.

He dug a **large** hole in the sand.

The word is **large**.

Spelling 4: The word is **spoons**.

We need **spoons** to eat our ice cream.

The word is **spoons**.

Spelling 5: The word is **hall**.

Class 2 played games in the **hall**.

The word is **hall**.

Spelling 6: The word is **crayons**.

She put all the red **crayons** in the pot.

The word is **crayons**.

Spelling 7: The word is **softest**.

This pillow is the **softest**.

The word is **softest**.

Spelling 8: The word is **shore**.

There were lots of shells on the **shore**.

The word is **shore**.

Spelling 9: The word is **kitchen**.

I left the cups in the **kitchen**.

The word is **kitchen**.

Spelling 10: The word is **rubbing**.

Ben was **rubbing** his eyes.

The word is **rubbing**.

Spelling 11: The word is **school**.

I was late for **school** on Monday.

The word is **school**.

Spelling 12: The word is **shiny**.

I saw a **shiny** gold ring on the grass.

The word is **shiny**.

Spelling 13: The word is **wrote**.

The children **wrote** on the paper.

The word is **wrote**.

Spelling 14: The word is **puddle**.

The rain made a big **puddle** on the floor.

The word is **puddle**.

Spelling 15: The word is **whiskers**.

My cat has very long **whiskers**.

The word is **whiskers**.

Spelling 16: The word is **worth**.

The vase was **worth** a lot of money.

The word is **worth**.

Spelling 17: The word is **carried**.

Mum **carried** the box down the stairs.

The word is **carried**.

Spelling 18: The word is **mention**.

Did you **mention** my name?

The word is **mention**.

Spelling 19: The word is **wear**.

Yuna has a new jumper to **wear**.

The word is **wear**.

Spelling 20: The word is **speechless**.

Dad was **speechless** when he saw the present.

The word is **speechless**.

Answers

Question	Spelling	Marks	Content domain
1	live	1m	S4: the /v/ sound at the end of words
2	fizz	1m	S1: the sounds /f/, /l/, /s/, /z/ and /k/ spelt *ff, ll, ss, zz* and *ck*
3	large	1m	S14: the /j/ sound is spelt *ge* at the end of words
4	spoons	1m	S8: spelling vowel digraphs; S5: adding *s* and *es* to nouns
5	hall	1m	S27: the /or/ sound spelt *a* before *l* and *ll*
6	crayons	1m	S8: spelling vowel digraphs; S5: adding *s* and *es* to nouns
7	softest	1m	S7: adding *–er* and *–est* to adjectives where no change is needed to the root word
8	shore	1m	S8: spelling vowel digraphs
9	kitchen	1m	S11: using *k* for the /k/ sound; S3: the /ch/ sound spelt *tch*
10	rubbing	1m	S26: adding *–ing, –ed, –er, –est* and *–y* to short words ending in a single consonant letter
11	school	1m	S37: common exception words
12	shiny	1m	S25: adding the endings *–ing, –ed, –er, –est* and *–y* to words ending in *–e*
13	wrote	1m	S17: the /r/ sound spelt *wr* at the beginning of words
14	puddle	1m	S18: adding *–le* at the end of words
15	whiskers	1m	S10: new consonant spellings *ph* and *wh*; S5: adding *s* and *es* to nouns
16	worth	1m	S31: the *or* spelling after *w*

Answers

Question	Spelling	Marks	Content domain
17	carried	1m	S24: adding –ed, –ing, –er and –est to a word ending consonant –y
18	mention	1m	S35: words ending in –tion
19	wear	1m	S36: homophones and near homophones; S8: vowel digraphs and trigraphs
20	speechless	1m	S34: the suffixes –ment, –ness, –ful, –less and –ly; S8: spelling vowel digraphs

End of English grammar, punctuation and spelling Paper 1 mark scheme

Answers   English GPS **Paper 2: grammar and punctuation**

Question	Content domain	Answer	Marks
Practice question a	G4.1d	helping ☑	0m
Practice question b	G3.2	Accept any appropriate adjective, for example: • **sunny** • **good**	0m
1	G5.3, G5.4	Award **1 mark** for **all** correctly matched. I can help you — ? How can I help — ! How helpful you are — .	1m
2	G3.3	Award **1 mark** for the correct option ticked. but ☑	1m
3	G5.1	Award **1 mark** for **all four** identified. (next) (tuesday) (megan) is going on holiday to (spain).	1m
4	G1.3	Award **1 mark** for the correct option ticked. an adjective ☑	1m
5	G6.3	Award **1 mark** for **all three** correct suffixes added. • bus**es** • sweet**s** • dish**es**	1m
6	G5.2	Award **1 mark** for the correct option ticked. full stop ☑	1m

Answers

Question	Content domain	Answer	Marks
7	G2.1, G2.3	Award **1 mark** for **all four** correct. 	Sentence	S	C	 Ruby is in the sandpit. → S ✓ Come and sit on the bench. → C ✓ Don't scare the ducks. → C ✓ I like playing on the swings. → S ✓	1m
8	G5.5	Award **1 mark** for the correct box ticked. I played football with Zahir Erin and Saskia this morning. (second box ticked ✓)	1m
9	G1	Award **1 mark** for the correct option ticked. a noun ✓	1m
10	G1.2	Award **1 mark** for **all three** identified. It (was) breakfast time and Tom (ate) his toast as Dad (hung) the washing on the line.	1m
11	G4.1a, G4.2	Award **1 mark** for the correct option ticked. The dog ran to the gate and barked. ✓	1m
12	G1.6	Award **1 mark** for the correct option ticked. kindly ✓	1m
13	G3.4	Award **1 mark** for the correct option ticked. because ✓	1m
14	G5.8	Award **1 mark** for: • **didn't**	1m

Answers

Question	Content domain	Answer	Marks
15	G4.1d, G4.2	Award **1 mark** for an answer in the present tense, for example: • **are** • **like** • **enjoy** **Do not accept** answers that are not in the present tense, for example: • **liked**	1m
16	G6.3	Award **1 mark** for the correct suffix circled. (ness)	1m
17	G4.1a	Award **1 mark** for **both** correct verbs: • **saw** • **chased**	1m
18	G5.8	Award **1 mark** for the correct option ticked. I've found Katie's shoes. ✓	1m
19	G2.2, G5.1, G5.3	Award **2 marks** for an appropriate, grammatically correct question with the correct punctuation, for example: • **Where have you been?** • **Did you have a good time?** • **Is your hair wet?** • **What did you do at the pool?** Award **1 mark** for an appropriate, grammatically correct question with incorrect punctuation, for example: • **Was the water cold.** • **do you like swimming?** • **Can you swim yet** • **How was your Swimming Lesson today?** **Do not accept** other sentence types, for example: • Dry your hair. • You are a good swimmer.	Up to 2m

End of English grammar and punctuation Paper 2 mark scheme

Schofield&Sims

Published by **Schofield & Sims Ltd**, 7 Mariner Court, Wakefield, West Yorkshire WF4 3FL, UK
Telephone 01484 607080
www.schofieldandsims.co.uk

This edition copyright © Schofield & Sims Ltd, 2020
First published in 2020

Authors: **Carol Matchett** and **Hilary Koll and Steve Mills**.
Carol Matchett and Hilary Koll and Steve Mills have asserted their moral rights under the Copyright, Designs and Patents Act, 1988, to be identified as the authors of this work.

British Library Cataloguing in Publication Data
A catalogue record for this book is available from the British Library.

Design by **Ledgard Jepson Ltd**
Front cover design by **Ledgard Jepson Ltd**

Printed in the UK by **Page Bros (Norwich) Ltd**

ISBN 978 07217 1652 7

Schofield & Sims KS1 SATs Practice Papers

English grammar, punctuation and spelling

Paper 2: grammar and punctuation

First name	
Middle name	
Last name	

Date of birth	Day		Month		Year	

School name	

Schofield&Sims

Total marks

Instructions

This is **English GPS Paper 2: grammar and punctuation**. It will test your grammar and punctuation skills. When you are ready to start, find a quiet place where you can concentrate.

Paper 2 contains 19 questions. Each question has a space for you to add your answer. You will start with practice questions.

For some questions, you will tick a box, circle your answer or draw lines to match answers. For other questions, you will write a word, phrase or sentence on a line.

You should read each question carefully before you answer it. Don't worry if you make a mistake. Simply put a line through it and write your new answer beside it.

Try your best to answer all of the questions in this paper. If you can't answer a question, move on to the next one and come back to it later.

This paper will take about **20 minutes**. Your adult helper will tell you when to start and when to stop. If you finish early, go back and check your work carefully.

Practice questions

a   Tick the word that completes this sentence.

I am _____ Harry.

Tick **one**.

help	☐
helped	☐
helping	☐
helps	☐

b   Write **one** word on the line below to complete the **noun phrase** in this sentence.

Saturday was a _____ day.

1 Draw lines to show the **punctuation mark** needed to complete each sentence. One has been done for you.

I can help you	•	•	?

How can I help	•	•	!

How helpful you are	•	•	.

1 mark

2 Tick the correct word to complete the sentence below.

Ellie wanted to go swimming _____ she forgot her towel.

Tick **one**.

and ☐

but ☐

or ☐

so ☐

1 mark

3 Circle **all** the words in the sentence below that must have a **capital letter**.

next tuesday megan is going on holiday to spain .

1 mark

4 What type of word is underlined in the sentence below?

The boy put on his <u>baggy</u> jumper.

Tick one.

a noun ☐

a verb ☐

an adjective ☐

an adverb ☐

1 mark

5 Add the suffix **s** or **es** to make each word a plural.

bus_____

sweet_____

dish_____

1 mark

6 Look at where the arrow is pointing.

We waited in the park all morning Jake was late.

Which **punctuation mark** is missing?

Tick **one**.

comma ☐

question mark ☐

full stop ☐

exclamation mark ☐

1 mark

7 Tick to show whether each sentence is a **statement** or a **command**.

Sentence	Statement	Command
Ruby is in the sandpit.		
Come and sit on the bench.		
Don't scare the ducks.		
I like playing on the swings.		

1 mark

8 Tick **one** box to show where a **comma** should go in the sentence below.

I played football with Zahir Erin and Saskia this morning.

☐ ☐ ☐ ☐

1 mark

9 What type of word is <u>fence</u> in the sentence below?

A bird sat on the wooden fence singing happily.

Tick one.

an adjective ☐

an adverb ☐

a noun ☐

a verb ☐

1 mark

10 Circle the **three verbs** in the sentence below.

It   was   breakfast   time   and   Tom   ate   his   toast

as   Dad   hung   the   washing   on   the   line.

1 mark

11 Tick the sentence that is correct.

Tick **one**.

The dog ran to the gate and bark.

☐

The dog ran to the gate and barks.

☐

The dog ran to the gate and barked.

☐

The dog run to the gate and barked.

☐

1 mark

12 Tick **one** box to show which word is an **adverb**.

The old lady spoke kindly to the little girl.

☐   ☐   ☐   ☐

1 mark

13 Tick the word that best completes the sentence below.

I chose this scarf _____ I liked the colour.

Tick one.

if ☐

that ☐

because ☐

when ☐

1 mark

14 Write the words <u>did not</u> as **one** word, using an **apostrophe**.

I _____ see you hiding in the corner.

1 mark

15 Write **one** word on the line below to complete the sentence in the **present tense**.

The children _____ helping Mrs Jackson.

1 mark

16 Circle the **suffix** needed to complete the word <u>dark</u> in the sentence below.

A tiger hid in the dark_____ of the forest.

er   ly   ness   ment

1 mark

17 The verbs in the boxes are in the present tense. Write these verbs in the **past tense**.

Lily _____ her friend and _____ after him.

1 mark

sees

chases

18 Tick the sentence that has the correct punctuation.

Tick **one**.

I've found Katies shoes. ☐

Ive found Katie's shoes. ☐

I've found Katie's shoes. ☐

Iv'e found Katie's shoes. ☐

1 mark

19 Molly comes home from the swimming pool.

Write a question that Mum might ask her. Remember to use the correct punctuation.

_____

2 marks

End of test

Published by **Schofield & Sims Ltd**, 7 Mariner Court, Wakefield, West Yorkshire WF4 3FL, UK
Telephone 01484 607080
www.schofieldandsims.co.uk

Authors: **Carol Matchett** and **Hilary Koll and Steve Mills**.
Carol Matchett and Hilary Koll and Steve Mills have asserted their moral rights under the Copyright, Designs and Patents Act, 1988, to be identified as the authors of this work.

British Library Cataloguing in Publication Data
A catalogue record for this book is available from the British Library.

Design by **Ledgard Jepson Ltd**
Front cover design by **Ledgard Jepson Ltd**

Printed in the UK by **Page Bros (Norwich) Ltd**

ISBN 978 07217 1652 7

Schofield & Sims KS1 SATs Practice Papers

English
grammar, punctuation and spelling

Paper 1: spelling

First name	
Middle name	
Last name	

Date of birth	Day		Month		Year	

School name	

This spelling test contains 20 different sentences. Each sentence has a word missing.

Your adult helper will use the script in the **Notes and answers** booklet. They will read out the word, then the sentence, then the word on its own again. You will start with a practice question.

Carefully fill in each missing word when it is read aloud.

You have **approximately 15 minutes** to complete this paper.

Schofield & Sims

Total marks

P   I fed the ducks in the _____ .

---

1   Some fish _____ in the sea.

2   The drink began to _____ .

3   He dug a _____ hole in the sand.

4   We need _____ to eat our ice cream.

5   Class 2 played games in the _____ .

6   She put all the red _____ in the pot.

7   This pillow is the _____ .

8   There were lots of shells on the _____ .

9   I left the cups in the _____ .

10   Ben was _____ his eyes.

11 I was late for _____ on Monday.

12 I saw a _____ gold ring on the grass.

13 The children _____ on the paper.

14 The rain made a big _____ on the floor.

15 My cat has very long _____ .

16 The vase was _____ a lot of money.

17 Mum _____ the box down the stairs.

18 Did you _____ my name?

19 Yuna has a new jumper to _____ .

20 Dad was _____ when he saw the present.

End of test

Published by **Schofield & Sims Ltd**, 7 Mariner Court, Wakefield, West Yorkshire WF4 3FL, UK
Telephone 01484 607080
www.schofieldandsims.co.uk

Authors: **Carol Matchett** and **Hilary Koll and Steve Mills**.
Carol Matchett and Hilary Koll and Steve Mills have asserted their moral rights under the Copyright, Designs and Patents Act, 1988, to be identified as the authors of this work.

British Library Cataloguing in Publication Data
A catalogue record for this book is available from the British Library.

Design by **Ledgard Jepson Ltd**
Front cover design by **Ledgard Jepson Ltd**

Printed in the UK by **Page Bros (Norwich) Ltd**

ISBN 978 07217 1652 7

Maths

Paper 1: arithmetic

First name	
Middle name	
Last name	

Date of birth	Day		Month		Year	

School name	

This is **Maths Paper 1**. It will test your arithmetic skills. When you are ready to start, find a quiet place where you can concentrate.

Paper 1 contains 25 questions. Each question has a box for you to add your answer. There is also space for your working out.

Your adult helper will help you with the practice question. Then you will do the other questions on your own.

You should read each question carefully before you answer it. Don't worry if you make a mistake. Simply put a line through it and write your new answer beside it.

Try your best to answer all of the questions. If you can't answer a question, move on to the next one and come back to it later.

This paper will take about **20 minutes**. Your adult helper will tell you when to start and when to stop. If you finish early, go back and check your work carefully.

Practice question

Work out the answer and write it in the black box. If you need to, use the space underneath for your working out.

$8 + 8 =$ ⬜

1 4 + 3 = ☐

1 mark

2 10 + 10 + 10 = ☐

1 mark

3   17 − 7 =

4   26 + 10 =

5   19 − 5 = ▭

1 mark

6   6 + 2 + 4 = ▭

1 mark

7   57 − 4 = ☐

8   37 + 6 = ☐

9   43 − 27 = [ ]

10   78 − 30 = [ ]

11   60 – 16 = ⬚

1 mark

12   6 × 5 = ⬚

1 mark

13 84 − 33 = ⬚

1 mark

14 100 ÷ 10 = ⬚

1 mark

15

$\boxed{} + 4 = 9$

16

$\boxed{} + 7 = 26$

1 mark

17 $\frac{1}{2}$ of 26 = [   ]

1 mark

18 $\frac{3}{4}$ of 20 = [   ]

1 mark

19   73 − ⬚ = 41

20   60 − ⬚ = 20

21   58 + 27 = ⬚

22   1 + 8 + 7 = ⬚

23 $\frac{1}{3}$ of 18 = [_____]

1 mark

24   50 ÷ 5 = [_____]

1 mark

25 68 – 19 = [ ]

1 mark

End of test

Published by **Schofield & Sims Ltd**, 7 Mariner Court, Wakefield, West Yorkshire WF4 3FL, UK
Telephone 01484 607080
www.schofieldandsims.co.uk

Authors: **Carol Matchett** and **Hilary Koll and Steve Mills**.
Carol Matchett and Hilary Koll and Steve Mills have asserted their moral rights under the Copyright, Designs and Patents Act, 1988, to be identified as the authors of this work.

British Library Cataloguing in Publication Data
A catalogue record for this book is available from the British Library.

Design by **Ledgard Jepson Ltd**
Front cover design by **Ledgard Jepson Ltd**

Printed in the UK by **Page Bros (Norwich) Ltd**

ISBN 978 07217 1652 7

Schofield & Sims KS1 SATs Practice Papers

Maths

Paper 2: reasoning

First name	
Middle name	
Last name	

Date of birth	Day		Month		Year	

School name	

Schofield&Sims

Total marks

This is **Maths Paper 2**. It will test your reasoning skills. When you are ready to start, find a quiet place where you can concentrate.

Paper 2 contains 31 questions. Most questions have a box for you to add your answer. For some questions, you will circle or draw lines to show the correct answer. You can use any blank space on the page for your working out.

Your adult helper will help you with the practice question. Then you will do the other questions on your own. The practice question and the first five questions will be read to you by your adult helper.

You should read each question carefully before you answer it. Don't worry if you make a mistake. Simply put a line through it and write your new answer beside it.

Try your best to answer all of the questions in this paper. If you can't answer a question, move on to the next one and come back to it later.

This paper will take about **35 minutes**. Your adult helper will tell you when to start and when to stop. If you finish early, go back and check your work carefully.

Practice question

berries

1

2

3

5

days

1 mark

Please do not start answering the questions on page 5 until you are told to do so.

6 Look at these cards.

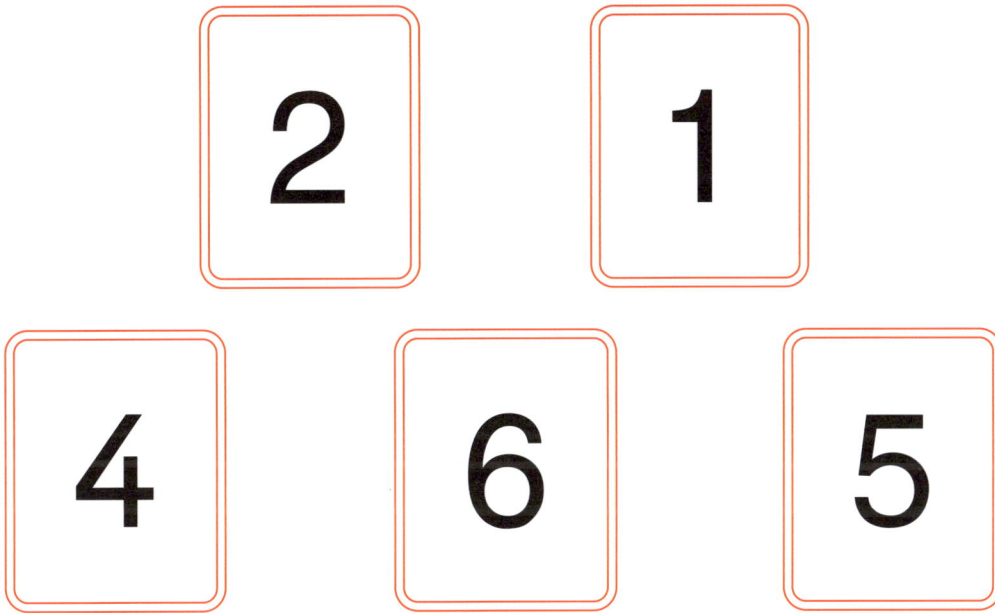

2	1

4	6	5

These two cards make a number **more than 60**.

6	5

Pick two cards to make a number **less than 15**.

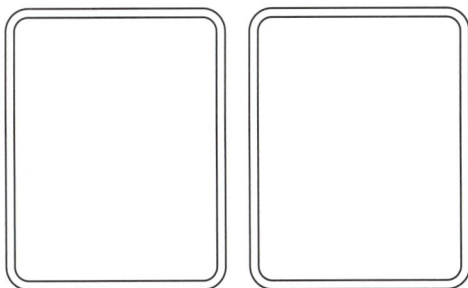

1 mark

7 Write a number in the box to make this subtraction correct.

$20 - 10 = 15 - $ ☐

1 mark

8 These numbers are not in order.

| 41 | ~~12~~ | 36 | 60 | 27 |

Write the numbers in order.

One has been done for you.

| 12 | ☐ | ☐ | ☐ | ☐ |

smallest   largest

1 mark

9 A watch costs **£45**.

Sam has **£28**.

How much **more** money does Sam need to buy the watch?

£ [   ]

10 Yusuf puts **5** pencils in each pot.

How many pencils are there **altogether**?

[   ] **pencils**

11 Look at these odd and even numbers.

Odd numbers	Even numbers
17	15
31	42
25	12
23	30

Circle the number that is in the wrong place.

1 mark

12 Write the missing numbers.

6	16		36	

1 mark

13 Jamal eats half of these biscuits.

How many biscuits does he eat?

biscuits

1 mark

14 There are **10** sweets in each bag.

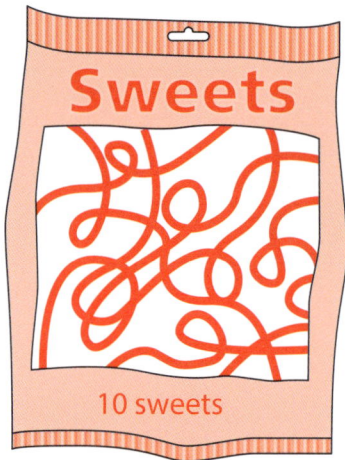

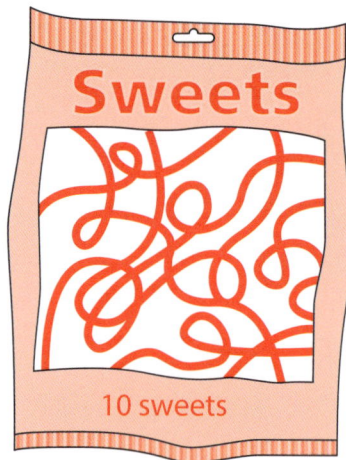

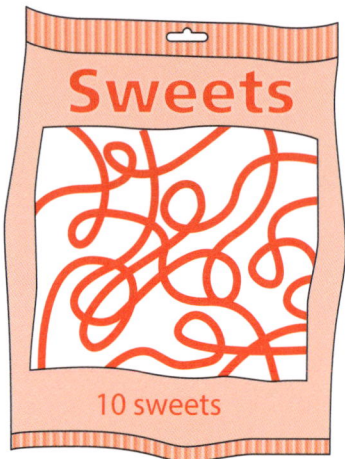

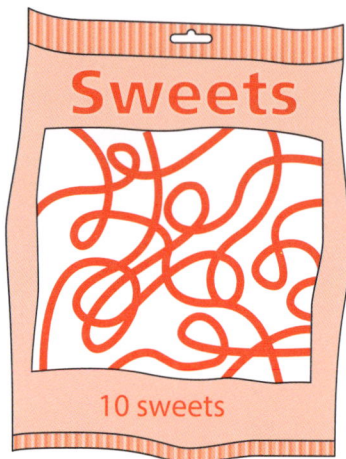

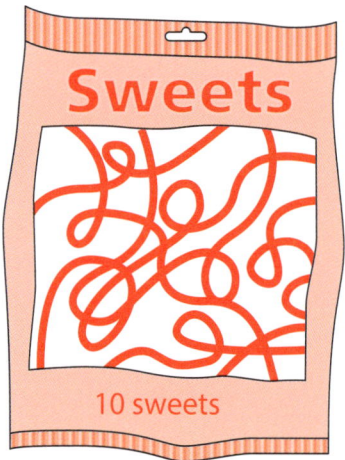

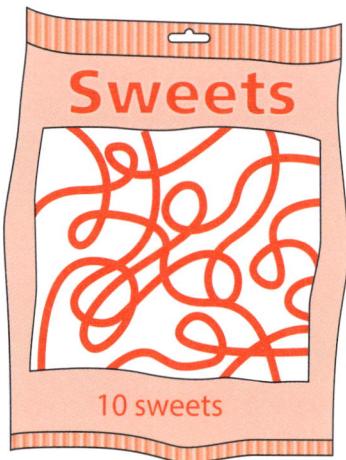

How many sweets are there **altogether**?

sweets

1 mark

15 Here are the prices of some ice creams.

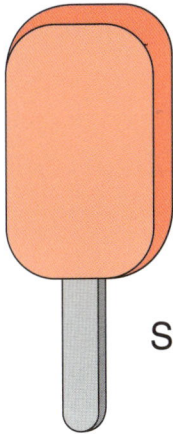

Strawberry 35p

Star 45p

Two scoops
55p

One scoop
40p

Which **two** ice creams together cost **exactly £1**?

	and	

1 mark

16 Write the missing numbers.

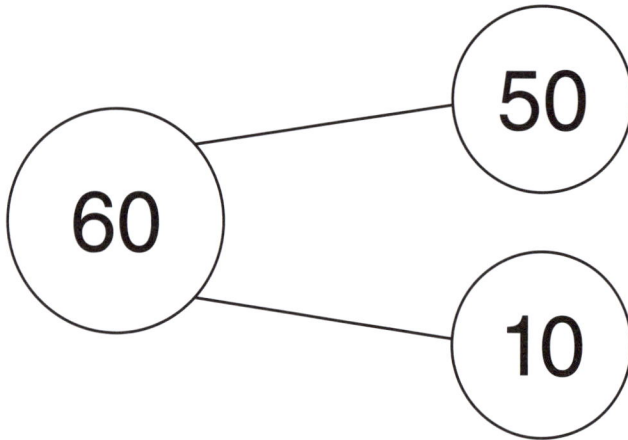

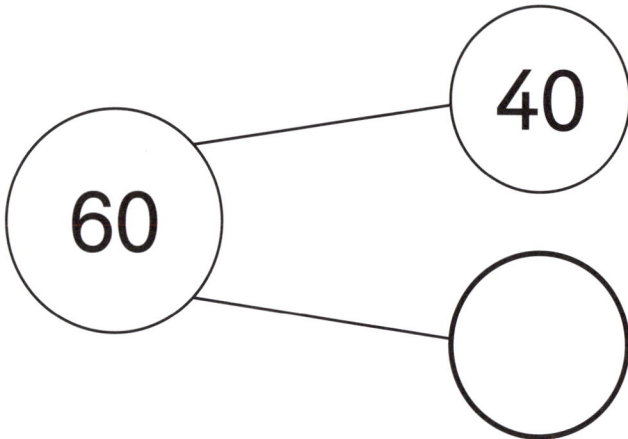

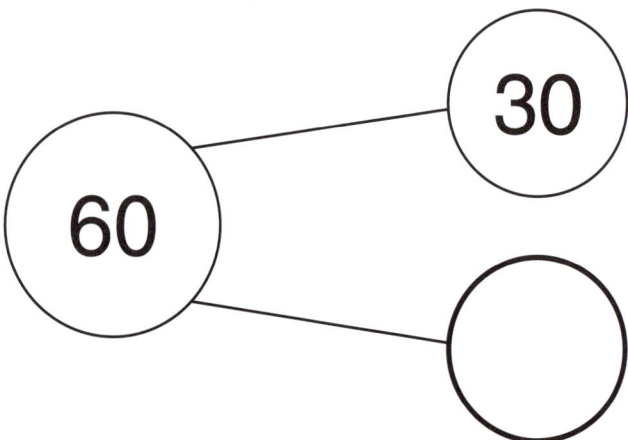

60 — 50
60 — 10

60 — 40
60 — ◯

60 — 30
60 — ◯

1 mark

17 How much juice is in the jug?

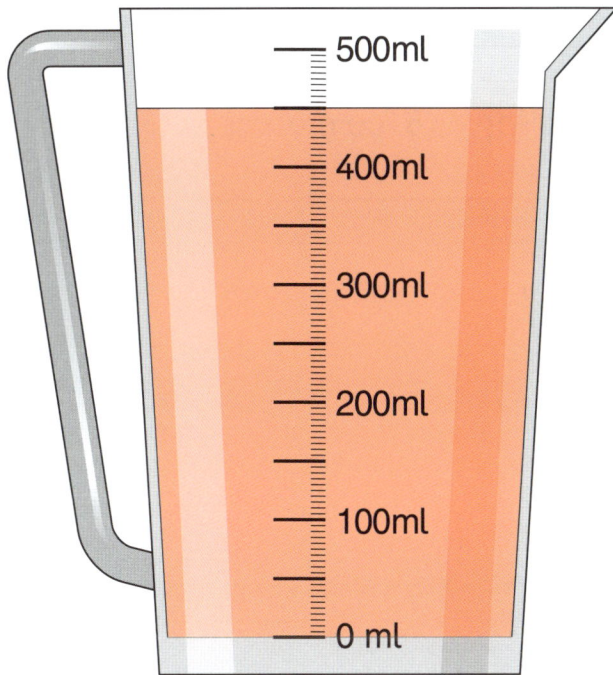

	ml

18 Here is part of a number pattern.

◯ ◯ ◯ ◯ ◯ ㊸ ㊹ ㊺

Where would **38** go?

Write **38** in the correct place.

19 Look at this pictogram.

Number of ice creams sold in one week

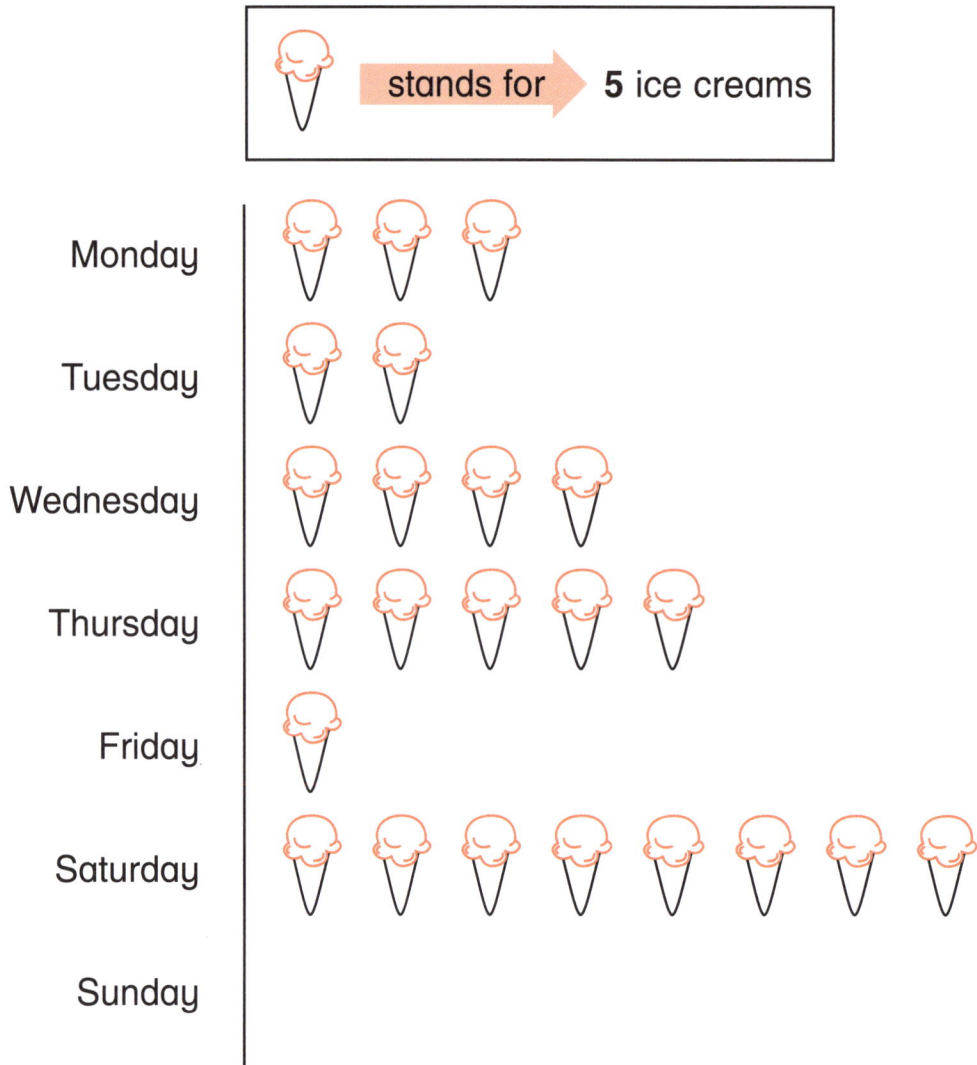

a) How many **more** ice creams were sold on Thursday than on Monday?

ice creams

1 mark

b) **5** ice creams were sold on **Sunday**.
Show this on the chart.

1 mark

20 Here are some sticks.

Circle the stick that is exactly **8cm** long.

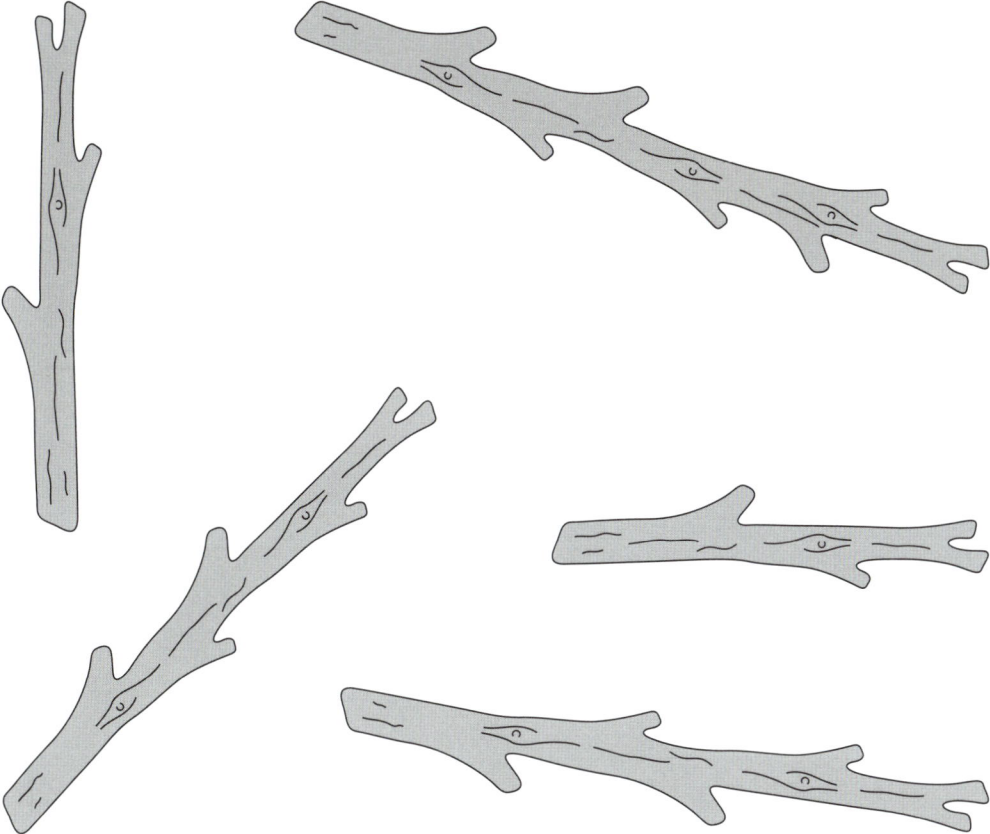

1 mark

21 Jen has **80p**.

She buys **2** apples and **1** banana.

20p

15p

How much money does Jen have **left**?

Show your working

p

2 marks

22 Tim and Raj have **10** strawberries.

They share them equally between themselves.

How many strawberries do they get each?

strawberries

_____
1 mark

23 Complete this number pattern.

64	half →	32	half →		half →		half →	

_____
1 mark

24 Tick the time that is shown on the clock.

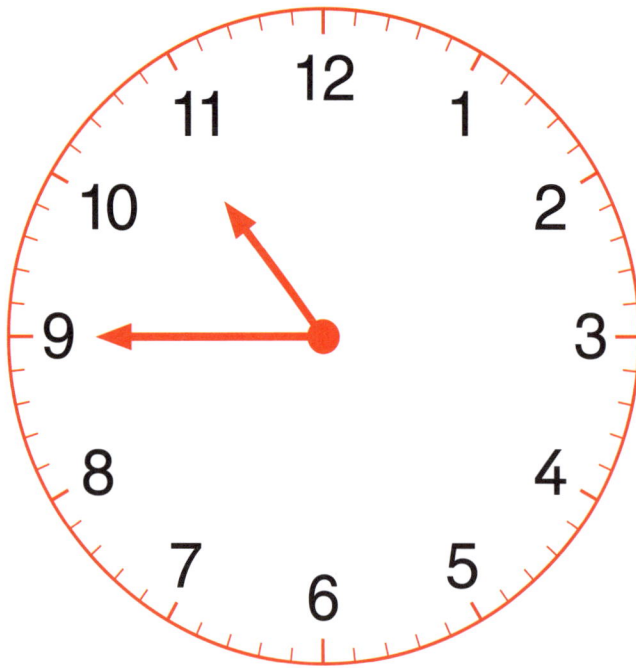

quarter to ten ☐   quarter to eleven ☐

quarter past ten ☐   quarter past eleven ☐

1 mark

Look at this trail.

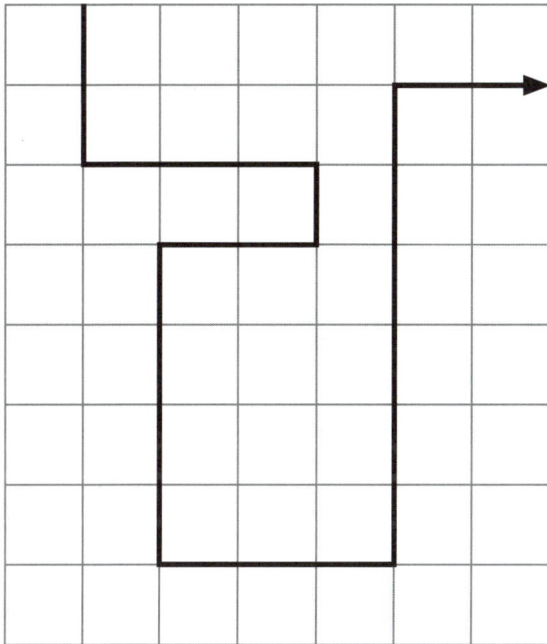

Complete these **instructions** for the trail.

down 2

right 3

down 1

26 What number do you think the down arrow is pointing to?

Write the number in the empty box.

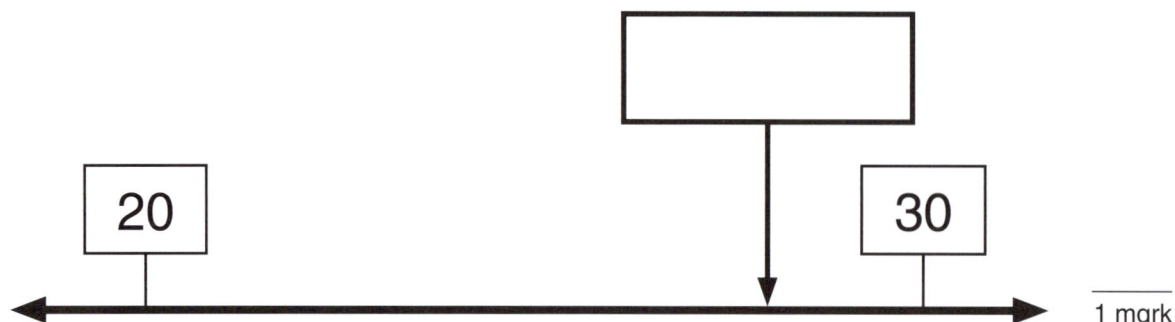

20	30

1 mark

27 Tick the shape with the **most** faces.

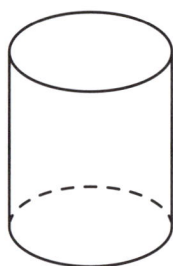

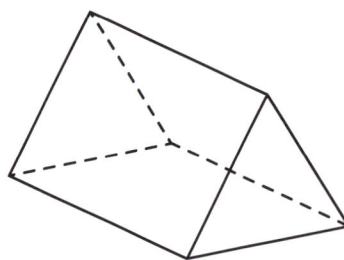

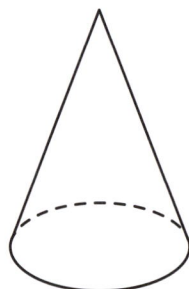

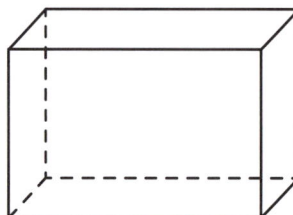

1 mark

28 Complete the calculations.

One has been done for you.

| 8 | ÷ | 2 | = | 4 |

| 10 | ÷ | 5 | = | |

| 30 | ÷ | | = | 3 |

_____
1 mark

29 Mrs Berry bakes cupcakes.

She sells them in her café.

On Saturday, she bakes **65** cupcakes and sells **36**.

How many does she have **left**?

| | cupcakes |

_____
1 mark

30 The scales are balanced.

The mass of each ball is **35** grams.

The mass of the feather is **25** grams lighter than a ball .

Find the mass of the toy car .

Show your working

_____ g

2 marks

31 Find the value of each symbol.

◯	◯	◯	6
△	◯	▢	13
5	4	10	

One has been done for you.

◯	=
▢	=
△	= 3

End of test

Published by **Schofield & Sims Ltd**, 7 Mariner Court, Wakefield, West Yorkshire WF4 3FL, UK
Telephone 01484 607080
www.schofieldandsims.co.uk

This edition copyright © Schofield & Sims Ltd, 2020
First published in 2020

Authors: **Carol Matchett** and **Hilary Koll and Steve Mills**.
Carol Matchett and Hilary Koll and Steve Mills have asserted their moral rights under the Copyright, Designs and Patents Act,
1988, to be identified as the authors of this work.

British Library Cataloguing in Publication Data
A catalogue record for this book is available from the British Library.

Design by **Ledgard Jepson Ltd**
Front cover design by **Ledgard Jepson Ltd**

Printed in the UK by **Page Bros (Norwich) Ltd**

ISBN 978 07217 1652 7

English reading

Paper 1: **Reading** prompt and answer booklet

First name	
Middle name	
Last name	
Date of birth	Day Month Year
School name	

Schofield&Sims

Total marks

Instructions

This is **English reading Paper 1**. It will test your reading comprehension skills. When you are ready to start, find a quiet place where you can concentrate.

Paper 1 contains 20 questions. Each question has a space for you to add your answer.

There are two texts to read. Read the first text and then answer the questions before you move on to the second text.

There is a list of 'Useful words' and two practice questions before each text. Your adult helper will help you with these questions. Then you will do the rest of the questions on your own.

For most questions, you will write your answer on the line or choose the right answer and tick the box next to it. For other questions, you will need to put numbers in boxes to order events or draw lines to match answers.

You should read each question carefully before you answer it. Don't worry if you make a mistake. Simply put a line through it and write your new answer beside it.

Try your best to answer all of the questions in this paper. If you can't answer a question, move on to the next one and come back to it later.

This paper will take about **30 minutes**. Your adult helper will tell you when to start and when to stop. If you finish early, go back and check your work carefully.

Contents

Useful words

jackal

dye

washerman

The Blue Jackal

A story from India

Once, a jackal went looking for food. He could not find anything to eat in the forest, so he went into the nearby village. It was midnight and everyone was asleep.

Practice questions

a Why did the jackal go into the village?

Tick **one**.

He was tired. ☐

He was lost. ☐

He was looking for food. ☐

He was late. ☐

b What time of day was it?

_____

Please do not start answering the questions on page 6 until you are told to do so.

The jackal saw an open window in a washerman's house. He peeped inside and saw lots of pots. "There must be something to eat in those pots," he said to himself.

He jumped down into the house, but...

Splash!

He landed in a tub full of blue dye left beneath the window.

He climbed out, but his fur was now bright blue! He tried to lick himself clean but the blue dye would not come off.

---

1 What did the jackal think was in the pots he saw?

_____

2 Where was the tub of blue dye?

Tick one.

outside the washerman's house	☐
by the door	☐
under the window	☐
on the fire	☐

Slowly, the jackal made his way back to the forest. "I do not look like a jackal now," he sighed sadly. "Everyone will laugh at me."

But all the other animals were amazed when they saw the blue jackal.

"What is this animal?" they asked.

"It must be some strange new beast," they said.

And they all ran away in terror.

3   Why was the jackal upset about his blue fur?

_____

1 mark

4   **Find** and **copy** the word that tells you the other animals were frightened by the blue jackal.

_____

1 mark

When the jackal saw all the animals running away, he had a clever idea. The jackal smiled to himself.

He called back all the frightened animals and said, "Oh beasts of the forest, blue is the colour of kings. From today, I am your king."

All the animals bowed down. "You are our king!" they said.

"What a grand colour I am," smiled the blue jackal.

---

5 How did the jackal feel when he saw the other animals running away?

Tick one.

sad ☐

upset ☐

pleased ☐

angry ☐

1 mark

6 What did the animals do after the blue jackal spoke to them?

_____

1 mark

7 Why did the jackal say "What a grand colour I am"?

_____

_____

1 mark

The jackal made all the animals serve him.

The lions and tigers hunted for his food. The elephants fetched his water. The mice found soft grass for him to sleep on. The birds sang for him. The monkeys fanned him with leaves.

The jackal just sat on his forest throne.

8 The jackal made all the animals serve him. Draw lines to show how each of the animals served him.

lions	•	•	fetched grass for his bed
mice	•	•	fanned him
elephants	•	•	found his food
monkeys	•	•	gave him water

1 mark

But the blue jackal would not go near the other jackals. He wanted nothing to do with them. He feared they knew his secret.

One day, he heard the other jackals talking. "He may be blue, but he is still only a jackal like us," they said. "The other animals spoil him."

At once, the blue jackal told the tigers to chase the other jackals out of the forest.

---

9 Why was the blue jackal worried about the other jackals?

_____

1 mark

10 What did the other jackals say about the blue jackal?

Tick one.

He was treated too well. ☐

He was treated badly. ☐

He was a special jackal. ☐

He was a good friend. ☐

1 mark

Many moons later, the jackals were sitting on a faraway hillside howling at the stars.

In the forest, the blue jackal heard them howling. Without thinking, he sat up and began to howl back just like any other jackal.

When the other animals heard that howl, they knew at once he was just a plain old jackal.

"This jackal has fooled us," the lion said. "He must be punished."

They chased the blue jackal away and he was never seen in the forest again.

11 ...*they knew at once he was just a plain old jackal.*
What does the word 'plain' mean in this sentence.

Tick **one**.

not pretty ☐

not clever ☐

not blue ☐

not special ☐

1 mark

12 The animals punished the jackal because...

Tick **one**.

he was different from them. ☐

he was a bad king. ☐

he pretended to be something he was not. ☐

he was dyed blue. ☐

1 mark

13 Number the sentences below from 1 to 4 to show the order they happen in the story.

The first one has been done for you.

The jackal returned to the forest. ☐

The jackal's fur was dyed blue. 1

The jackal was chased out of the forest. ☐

The jackal tricked the other animals. ☐

1 mark

Please turn over to the next page.

Please do not start answering the questions on page 16 until you are told to do so.

Useful words

Antarctic

emperor penguins

ocean

Penguins

Penguins are amazing birds. They live in the Antarctic in a land of snow and ice. They cannot fly, but they are superb swimmers.

Practice questions

c Where do penguins live?

_____

d What do penguins do very well?

Tick **one**.

fly ☐

sing ☐

swim ☐

ski ☐

Please do not start answering the questions on page 16 until you are told to do so.

On land, penguins stand upright and waddle about. Some penguins find that the best way to travel across the snowy land is to slide on their fat bellies using their wings to push and steer.

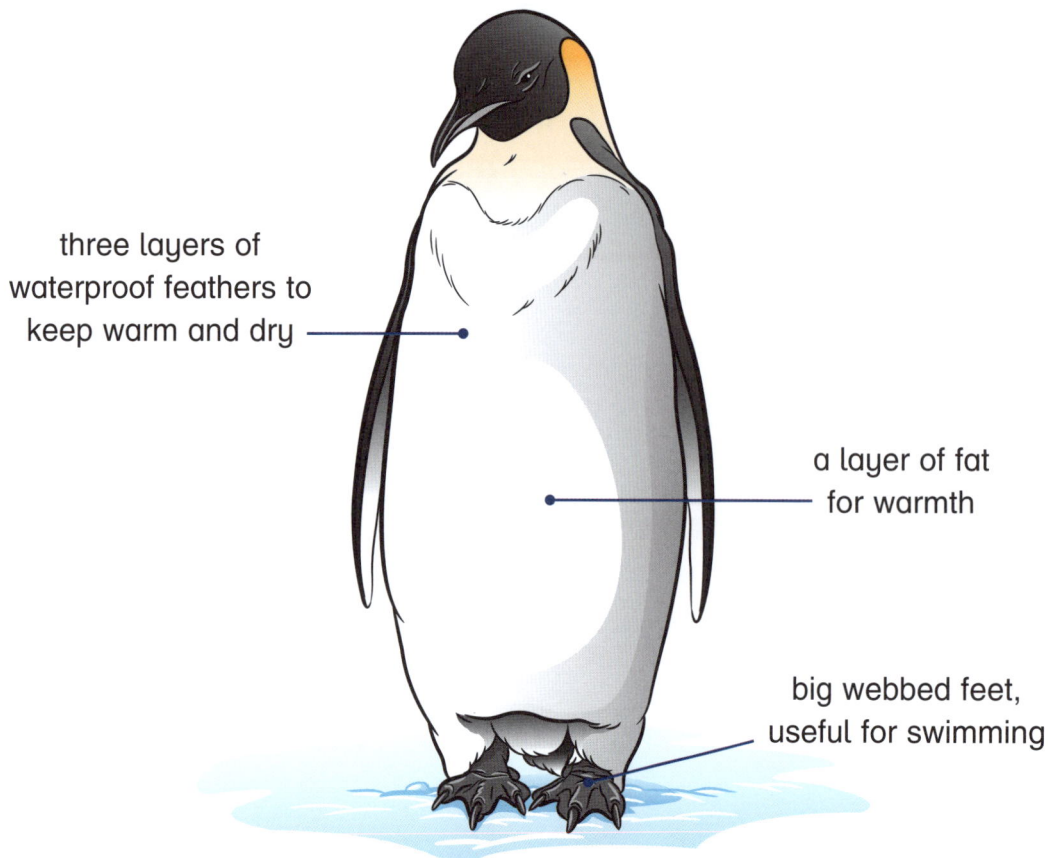

three layers of waterproof feathers to keep warm and dry

a layer of fat for warmth

big webbed feet, useful for swimming

14 How do some penguins use their wings to help them travel on land?

Tick **one**.

to help them fly ☐ to help them walk ☐

to help them swim ☐ to help them slide ☐

1 mark

15 Give **two** parts of the body that help to keep the penguin warm.

1. _____

2. _____

1 mark

Penguins can dive deep down into the ocean. They catch all their food underwater and need to swim very fast. They use their wings as flippers to help them glide through the water. Their spiky tongues help grip the slippery fish.

16 Which word in the text describes what the penguin's tongue is like?

Tick **one**.

slippery ☐   grip ☐

spiky ☐   glide ☐

1 mark

17 Why do penguins need to swim fast?

_____

1 mark

In spring, emperor penguins walk far across the snow and ice to lay their eggs. The mother penguin then waddles off to the sea to find food. The father stays and takes care of the egg. Emperor penguins do not build nests so for two months the father balances the egg on his feet, keeping it off the ice. He keeps the egg tucked under a cosy flap of skin.

18   Which of the following sentences is **true**?

Tick **one**.

Emperor penguins build nests in spring. ☐

Emperor penguins lay eggs in spring. ☐

The mother penguin takes care of the egg. ☐

The father penguin goes to find food. ☐

1 mark

19 Why must the penguin keep the egg off the ice?

_____ 1 mark

20 **Find** and **copy** a word that tells you the egg is warm under the flap of skin.

_____ 1 mark

End of test

Published by **Schofield & Sims Ltd**, 7 Mariner Court, Wakefield, West Yorkshire WF4 3FL, UK
Telephone 01484 607080
www.schofieldandsims.co.uk

This edition copyright © Schofield & Sims Ltd, 2020
First published in 2020

Authors: **Carol Matchett** and **Hilary Koll and Steve Mills**.
Carol Matchett and Hilary Koll and Steve Mills have asserted their moral rights under the Copyright, Designs and Patents Act, 1988, to be identified as the authors of this work.

British Library Cataloguing in Publication Data
A catalogue record for this book is available from the British Library.

Design by **Ledgard Jepson Ltd**
Front cover design by **Ledgard Jepson Ltd**

Printed in the UK by **Page Bros (Norwich) Ltd**

ISBN 978 07217 1652 7

English reading

Paper 2: Reading answer booklet

First name	
Middle name	
Last name	
Date of birth	Day ___ Month ___ Year ___
School name	

Total marks

[Blank page]

This is **English reading Paper 2**. It will test your reading comprehension skills. When you are ready to start, find a quiet place where you can concentrate.

Paper 2 contains 18 questions. Each question has a space for you to add your answer.

For this paper, there is a separate Reading booklet containing three reading texts: one fiction text, one poem and one non-fiction text. Read each text and then answer the questions before you move on to the next text.

For most questions, you will write your answer on the line or choose the right answer and tick the box next to it. For other questions, you will need to tick to show if a statement is true or false, or draw lines to match answers.

You should read each question carefully before you answer it. Don't worry if you make a mistake. Simply put a line through it and write your new answer beside it.

Try your best to answer all of the questions in this paper. If you can't answer a question, move on to the next one and come back to it later.

This paper will take about **40 minutes**. Your adult helper will tell you when to start and when to stop. If you finish early, go back and check your work carefully.

1 Why did the Cloud-Eater live at the top of a tall mountain? (page 4)

_____

1 mark

2 **Find** and **copy two** words that describe how dry the ground was. (page 4)

1. _____

2. _____

1 mark

3 Why did the boy decide to try to kill the Cloud-Eater? (page 4)

_____

1 mark

4 Why was the boy's grandmother proud of him? (page 5)

_____

1 mark

5 How did the boy find his way easily up the mountain? (page 5)

_____

1 mark

6 How did the boy know that he was near enough to the Cloud-Eater to fire the arrow? (page 6)

_____

1 mark

7 The feathers helped the boy to defeat the Cloud-Eater.
Draw lines to match the feathers to the help they gave him.

the red feather		helped him shrink in size
the blue feather		helped him find his way
the yellow feather		helped him fire the arrow
the black feather		helped him speak to the gopher

1 mark

8 Think about the whole story.

What do you think is likely to happen when the boy returns to the village?

I think _____

_____

_____

1 mark

9 Where is the bridge in the poem? (page 7)

Tick **one**.

over a pond ☐   over the sea ☐

over a river ☐   over a railway ☐

1 mark

10 Write **three** creatures that the writer wishes to see. (page 7)

1. _____

2. _____

3. _____

1 mark

11 *I want to see his great round eyes* (page 7)

What does the word 'great' mean in this line?

Tick **one**.

excellent	☐	many	☐
big	☐	important	☐

1 mark

12 The poet thinks of two things she would like to do while standing on the bridge. Explain what these two ideas are. (page 7)

1. _____

_____

2. _____

_____

2 marks

13 Why did people in Britain not eat tomatoes at first? (page 8)

_____

1 mark

14 Why are tomatoes sometimes grown in greenhouses? (page 8)

_____

1 mark

15 Give **three** ways to use uncooked tomatoes. (page 9)

1. _____

2. _____

3. _____

1 mark

16 The earliest ketchup was made from...

(page 10)

Tick **one**.

tomatoes ☐

peaches ☐

mushrooms ☐

fish ☐

1 mark

17 Every year, lots of people take part in the food festival 'La Tomatina'. What do they do there?

(page 10)

_____

1 mark

18 Put ticks in the table to show which sentences (pages 9–10)
are **true** and which are **false**.

Sentence	True	False
Tomatoes are vegetables.		
The bright colours in tomatoes are good for you.		
Today all tomatoes are red.		
Tomato leaves are not good to eat.		

2 marks

End of test

Published by **Schofield & Sims Ltd**, 7 Mariner Court, Wakefield, West Yorkshire WF4 3FL, UK
Telephone 01484 607080
www.schofieldandsims.co.uk

This edition copyright © Schofield & Sims Ltd, 2020
First published in 2020

Authors: **Carol Matchett** and **Hilary Koll and Steve Mills**.
Carol Matchett and Hilary Koll and Steve Mills have asserted their moral rights under the Copyright, Designs and Patents Act, 1988, to be identified as the authors of this work.

British Library Cataloguing in Publication Data
A catalogue record for this book is available from the British Library.

Design by **Ledgard Jepson Ltd**
Front cover design by **Ledgard Jepson Ltd**

Printed in the UK by **Page Bros (Norwich) Ltd**

ISBN 978 07217 1652 7

The Cloud-Eater

On the bridge

Tomatoes

Reading Booklet

Schofield & Sims KS1 SATs Practice Papers

Contents

The Cloud-Eater

The Cloud-Eater lived at the top of the tallest mountain. He craved for clouds and was always hungry. Every day, he stood on the mountain top, opened his enormous mouth and swallowed every cloud that floated by: white fluffy clouds, gloomy grey clouds and the dark clouds that carried rain. No cloud escaped the Cloud-Eater's gaping mouth.

With a cloudless sky, no rain fell in the valleys below. Soon the land was baked hard and the fields were scorched as dry as a bone. The crops shrivelled and the people began to starve.

The people knew they must destroy the Cloud-Eater but no-one volunteered to try.

Then a young boy heard his grandmother talking about the troubles and misery caused by the Cloud-Eater. The boy heard the sorrow in her voice and decided that he would go to kill the Cloud-Eater. "I will make the people happy," he said.

When his grandmother heard his plan, she felt proud of her grandson and gave him four feathers to take on his journey. "This red feather will guide you," she said. "The blue feather will let you speak the language of animals. The yellow feather will shrink you to the size of the tiniest creature. The black feather will give you strength and courage when you need it most."

The boy put the red feather in his headband and tucked the others safely in his belt. Off he went, finding the way easily through the maze of trails and hidden mountain paths. As the mountain grew steeper, the boy began to struggle in the sweltering heat. Suddenly, he noticed a strange furry little creature sitting by a hole in the ground. It was a gopher. The boy quickly put the blue feather in his headband and asked the gopher if he knew where to find the Cloud-Eater.

"Yes, my burrow goes so close to the Cloud-Eater that I can sometimes hear him snoring at night," said the gopher. "Follow me."

With that the gopher disappeared into the hole. The boy put the yellow feather in his headband and in a flash he was small enough to slip into the hole after the gopher.

The gopher scampered ahead and the boy followed close behind. The tunnel took them deeper and deeper into the mountain. Finally, they stopped in a place so close to the Cloud-Eater that they could hear his heart beating.

The boy put the black feather in his hair and took out his bow. Fearlessly, he placed an arrow in the bow, drawing it back. He took aim and sent the arrow speeding down the tunnel towards the Cloud-Eater. There was a tremendous roar and rumble. The mountain began to shake; rocks began to tumble. Finally, all was silent.

In the tunnel, the boy and the gopher cheered. Outside, around the mountain peak, clouds began to gather – white fluffy clouds, gloomy grey clouds and the dark clouds that carry rain. Soon the first drops of rain fell on the grateful land once more.

Mexican traditional story

On the bridge

If I could see a little fish –
That is what I just now wish;
I want to see his great round eyes
Always open in surprise.

I wish a water rat would glide
Slowly to the other side;
Or a dancing spider sit
On the yellow flags a bit.

I think I'll get some stones to throw,
And watch the pretty circles show.
Or shall we sail a flower-boat,
And watch it slowly – slowly float?

That's nice – because you never know
How far away it means to go;
And when to-morrow comes, you see,
It may be in the great wide sea.

Kate Greenaway

Tomatoes

History of the tomato

Tomatoes were first grown for food in southern Mexico thousands of years ago. They were called tomatl, which is where the word 'tomato' comes from.

Tomatoes first arrived in Europe in the sixteenth century, probably brought back by Spanish or Italian explorers.

The very first tomatoes were yellow, so they were named golden apples or pomi d'oro in Italian. The Italian for tomatoes today is pomodoro even though now most tomatoes are red.

To begin with, people in Britain grew tomatoes as decorative plants rather than for food. They thought the bright colour of tomatoes was a danger signal and they were poisonous.

Tomatoes growing in a greenhouse

Tomatoes today

Tomatoes today come in all shapes and sizes – from large beefsteak tomatoes to plum tomatoes and baby cherry tomatoes.

Tomatoes are now widely grown all over the world, even as far north as Iceland. In cooler countries, tomatoes are usually grown in greenhouses.

Fact: Tomato seedlings have even been grown in space.